WITH AN INTRODUCTION BY JOAN COLLINS

A Fireside Book

PUBLISHED BY SIMON & SCHUSTER, INC.

NEW YORK   LONDON   TORONTO   SYDNEY   TOKYO

Joan Collins

P O R T R A I T S

O F   A   S T A R

Copyright © 1987 by Edward Sanderson
A Fireside Book
Published by Simon & Schuster, Inc.
Simon & Schuster Building
Rockefeller Center
1230 Avenue of the Americas
New York, New York 10020
FIRESIDE and colophon are registered trademarks
of Simon & Schuster, Inc.
Designed by Bonni Leon
Manufactured in the United States of America
Printed and bound by Kingsport Press
10   9   8   7   6   5   4   3   2   1
Library of Congress Cataloging in Publication Data
Sanderson, Eddie.
Joan Collins: the lady in the lens.

"A Fireside book."
1. Collins, Joan—Portraits.
2. Moving-picture actors and actresses—Great Britain—
Portraits.   I. Title.
PN2598.C66S26   1987   791.43′028′0924   [B]   87-9517
ISBN: 0-671-63411-9

*M*y sincere and grateful thanks to Joan Collins for her indispensable help with this book, given so generously at a time when she was starring in "Dynasty," producing and starring in "Monte Carlo," appearing on talk shows, participating in promotional events, TV commercials, being involved with book projects, house moving . . . and so on.

Also, my wife, Lindy—for her suggestion that I do this book.

And to Judy Bryer, special thanks for her research and discovery of photographs that had long been absorbed into family collections.

7o Scott Sanderson
who slowed me down
enough to put this
book together.

*T*o Katy Kass
without whom
there would
be no page one.

Introduction by Joan Collins

Photography today is as much an art form as painting and filmmaking. To be able to find the essence of a person or object through the lens of a camera is a gift.

There are many great photographers throughout the world who depend on mood lighting, atmosphere, and certain kinds of props to capture a good photograph.

Eddie Sanderson depends only on his subject and the atmosphere of the moment. Naturally, he uses strobe and available light, but the photographs he has taken of me over the past fourteen years represent with accuracy moments in time. With a single shot he is able to capture situations as diverse as the chaos of moving house and the panic of being trapped in a Florida swamp surrounded by mud, snakes, and swamp creatures. And yet, when circumstances permit, he is particularly adept at putting his subject in the right frame of mind.

Fourteen years is a long time to be associated with one person whom you truly trust and respect. Obviously, when you work with somebody for that length of time you are at ease with him and have none of the apprehensions that you might have working with somebody new. Eddie and I are completely relaxed with each other and say exactly what we please. We've obviously had a few disagreements now and again but have been able to solve everything with an understanding chat.

*E*ddie has photographed me at least three or four times a year since 1972, from our first session in Marbella, Spain—when he was an eager young photographer with the London *Sunday Mirror* doing a story about my new baby, Katyana; husband, Ron Kass; two older children, Tara and Sacha; and Ron's three boys, Robert, David, and Jonathan—to our most recent one, a rough fight

scene with Diahann Carroll on the set of "Dynasty."

Each session has had its own particular quality, and with the exception of a few shoots such as the yearly Nolan Miller fashion parade of Alexis' couture, not one has been exactly like another.

When we work, we work hard. He does everything himself, without assistants; we work one to one, as I find I relate to the camera better if there are only the photographer, the camera, and me. I loathe those sessions when fifteen or twenty people not only stand around watching every move but often at the end of the session break out into embarrassing applause.

*S*ometimes Eddie suggests a premise for a photograph, sometimes I do. One I was most insistent upon but with which he totally disagreed revolved around some silver lamé curtains that I had brought to Los Angeles from

London and that I was rather fond of. I envisioned a photograph of myself in a gold lamé dress, lying on these curtains draped across a settee in my sitting room, à la some exotic 1920s movie star—a vision of gold and silver lamé.

Eddie vehemently disagreed with me. "That will look terrible!" he said. "A bunch of old silver curtains and you lying in a gold lamé frock. It'll look bloody awful."

"No it won't," I said.

"Yes it will," he said (he is almost as stubborn as I).

"All right," he said. "I'll do it, but it will be horrible."

"No it won't," said I.

We shot it, and it turned out to be one of the best glamour photographs we had done.

He in turn had to force me to pose for a session in 1979 in my house on Carolyn Way in Beverly Hills, surrounded by Bekins cardboard cartons, attempting to paint the kitchen—something I have not attempted before or since but which caused us much hilarity and showed a different side of me.

Not only is he a wonderful photographer but he is also one of my closest friends (his adorable five- year-old son, Scott, is my godson). I consider myself fortunate to have an association with a photographer whom I respect and who is honest with me. I know that if I stick out my tongue at the camera when he is taking a picture, it won't appear in print . . . wrong!

*C*ertainly, taking photographs has not been without stress. In Paris, in 1985, Eddie wanted some exclusive photographs for certain international publications during filming of the mini-series "Sins." However, he was dogged by an enthusiastic German photographer who tried to copy everything Eddie set up. Each time we found a quiet spot in the Gardens of Versailles or another great location, this young man would follow us and start snapping too. Eddie was becoming exasperated until he came up with an idea. "What about going to the Arc de Triomphe and shooting in the late afternoon at sunset?"

"Terrible idea," I said. "The place is swarming with tourists."

"I'll shoot really fast," he said. "You'll just jump

out of the car and walk down the middle of the traffic. It will take you twenty seconds and we'll have the pictures . . . bang . . . bang . . . and we won't have any other photographers around," he said smugly.

"All right," I said. "It's on our way to the hotel anyway."

Off we barreled in our black Citroën, braving Paris rush-hour traffic. Out I jumped at the Arc de Triomphe; out came Eddie's Nikons as I dodged speeding traffic into the center of the Champs-Elysées. Suddenly, a tiny car pulled up and out jumped the German friend, cameras poised to shoot. "Damn it," said Eddie, "can't we ever get away from you?"

Taking my hand, Eddie pulled me toward our car, keeping himself positioned between the photographer and me. As we reached the curb, Eddie stopped, saw the other photographer heading to his car, and said, "Let's grab one shot," and we did as I dashed through the traffic for the safety of the sidewalk. It turned out to be the best photo of that session.

*A*nother time, we were in Venice, Italy, and I was wearing an extremely tight eighteenth-century costume, with a very large wig. Eddie had taken at least nine million photographs, and I was rather fed up. "Don't you have enough?" I asked coldly.

"I want the exclusives, away from the company photographers," he demanded.

"This dress is extremely uncomfortable," I said.

"Oh, it looks great," he said.

"It's agony; it's tight, really heavy."

"How heavy?"

"I'll show you," I said. I went into my dressing room, took off the dress, and left it *standing* in the middle of the room by itself. "There, come in and see!" I said when I came out. "How would you like to wear *that* for twelve hours?"

"I love it!" he cried, and he actually took a picture of the dress.

I felt sorry for him, in Venice again, one night when we had taken a group of friends for a gondola ride along the canals. Suddenly, the heavens opened and everyone ducked for cover beneath the tarpaulins the gondoliers keep handy. Eddie thought this was a delicious picture and stayed out in the rain, hair and clothes plastered to his body, snapping away as lightning illuminated the canals and the rest of us snuggled beneath the tarpaulin.

*H*e has also taken several shots for my Xmas cards, the most ingenious being on a hot July afternoon in Los Angeles when we dressed six-year-old Katy in a red Santa Claus outfit and posed her in front of a wilting fir tree. I stood on a table throwing little cotton-wool balls at her while Eddie snapped away, determined to get the Xmas'y feeling, which is not easy in 95 degrees in July. But the picture was fabulous and really epitomized a child's ecstasy in the Xmas season.

I did my first semi-nude pictures for Eddie. In 1976, in Hollywood, I played the part of April in *The Moneychangers*. One of the scenes called for April to jump naked into a swimming pool. I had closed the set to all but the director and necessary crew, but Eddie, with his charming half-Scottish wheedling ways, persuaded me that he should stay to take the pictures of me. Well, he did . . . and I've been trying to burn the negatives ever since!

*O*ur most difficult working situation was, without doubt, shooting *Empire of the Ants* in the Florida swamps. But I think those are some of the most interesting photographs in terms of action, showing how unglamorous and arduous an actress's life can often be. In the pictures of me sitting in the middle of a swamp with cuts all over my legs, shivering with cold, and surrounded by all kinds of nasty swamp life, I was not acting!

We are both strong-willed people and have our own ideas about how things should be done.

One day he called up and said, "How do you look without makeup?"

"You know how I look without makeup," I said. "You've seen me a hundred times without makeup. How do you think I look?"

"I think you look great," he said.

"What do you want?" I asked suspiciously, knowing he was up to something.

"Well, one of the English newspapers would like to do a photograph of six actresses without their makeup to see what they really look like. Are you game?"

I thought about this for a while. "Who are the others?"

"Well, they can't find the other five yet, but I said I was sure you would do it, since you don't have that sort of vanity."

"Hmm!" I said, "I'll do it, as long as you don't mind being at the studio at six o'clock in the morning, which is the time we poor souls have to get there."

As it turned out, he couldn't find five other actresses who would consent to a stills session without their makeup on. I was the only fool who agreed—that's friendship for you.

I like Eddie's camera, and I think that if you like the camera, the camera usually likes you. It's not true that the camera never lies. The camera can lie, or it can certainly fib a bit. With the right lighting, the right makeup, and the right angles, it is possible to transform someone who doesn't feel like being photographed into someone who looks terrific. Eddie has been consistent in always making me look as good as possible and has hardly ever taken any photographs of me that I have not liked.

I love the photographs in this book—a cross section of material—a few slides of my life, and I hope everyone enjoys looking at them as much as we enjoyed making them.

Joan Collins

JC August 1986. Keeping Scott Sanderson, Eddie's son, amused at our new house in Beverly Hills. We hadn't moved in yet but spent several Sundays by the pool planning the interior renovation and design.

JC

This was my
favorite
picture at
the time.

JC At this stage of my life, I was moving a lot and all my bedrooms had the same green and white wallpaper.

ES Joan's superstardom was recognized in typically American fashion when she became the subject of one of Dean Martin's roasts. Barbs from the celebrity panel flew thick and fast. One of Phyllis Diller's one-liners: "By the time she was eighteen she had sown enough wild oats to make a grain deal with Russia."

JC Beauty shots at home. I liked this particular picture a lot and sent it out to fans for several years. ▲

JC I really don't think I have any special secret. I think it's a question of attitude and how you feel. I'm not a vegetarian or anything like that. I eat almost everything—except white bread, which is a killer. I also believe in allowing myself a lot of time to just flake out—no answering phones, no makeup, just resting, reading magazines, watching TV, being close friends with Katy.

 *JC* Actress/Photographer Julie Edge working in her boots and little else. Eddie thought he would take a glamorous photo of me in the Jacuzzi.

. . . I had other ideas.

We wish you a Merry Christmas

And a New Year of Peace and Prosperity

What a great photo!

A Christmas card, 1981. Katy was nine. It was our first
Christmas in the Century City apartment.

JC The hand that rocks the cradle also throws the snow.

ES Christmas in July. The temperature outside was close to ninety-five degrees Fahrenheit and the snow was cotton wool as we shot Joan's 1977 Christmas card.

merry christmas

JOAN AND RON KASS
TARA, SACHA AND KATYANA

Happy Holidays
From Our Own Dynasty

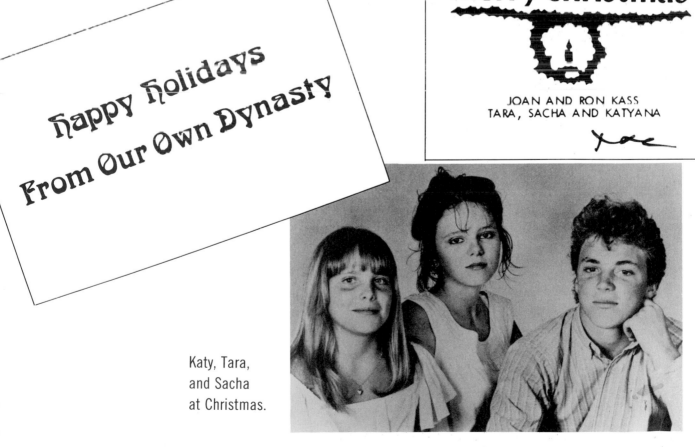

Katy, Tara, and Sacha at Christmas.

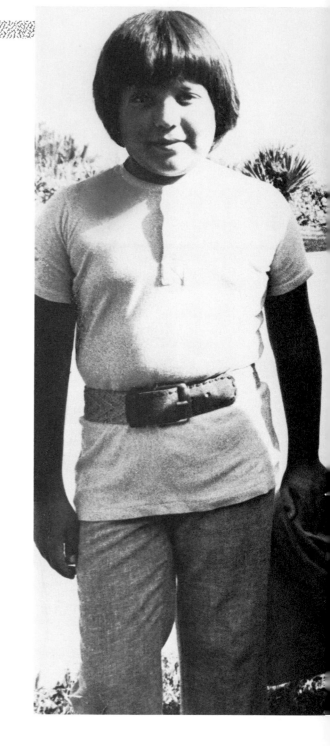

JC   We leased an apartment in Century City in 1981 for six months because that's how long I expected "Dynasty" to last. Here's Ron Kass, my third husband—a charming, amiable American. A really sweet guy. And the really great love of my life, my daughter Katy. She almost died a few years ago, but with love and prayer she survived. Now she's a real beauty.

JC "His, Hers, and Theirs." Easter 1972. Holiday home, Marbella, Spain. The very first picture ever taken of me.

ES The Swiss Family Kass. Combined families, Robert Kass (ten), Jonathan Kass (five), Katy Kass (six weeks), Tara Newly (eight), Sacha Newly (six), David Kass (twelve).

JC The master bedroom of the Bowmont house before I went to work on it. ▲

JC This is my future dining room. Once the chairs arrive, I'll be able to sit down! ▶

Bowmont sitting room. ▲

JC Family portrait shortly after we arrived in Los Angeles in 1975.

JC

I spend most of my
free time with my
daughter Katy.

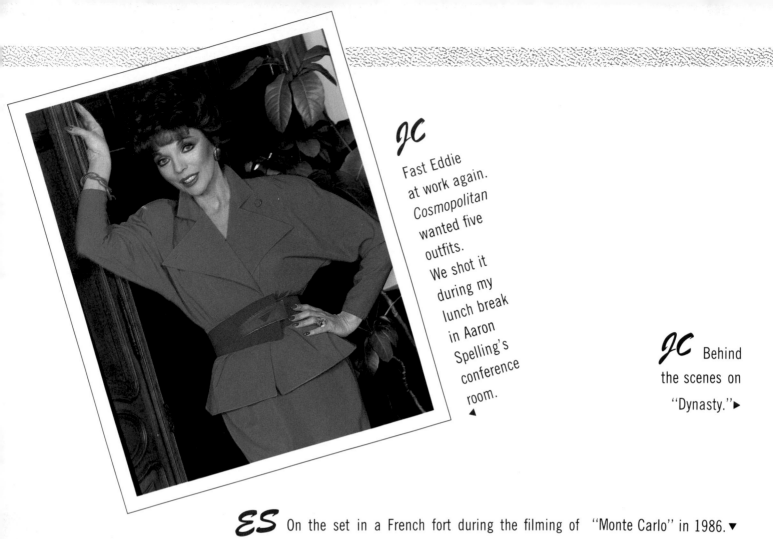

JC Fast Eddie at work again. *Cosmopolitan* wanted five outfits. We shot it during my lunch break in Aaron Spelling's conference room. ▲

JC Behind the scenes on "Dynasty." ▶

ES On the set in a French fort during the filming of "Monte Carlo" in 1986. ▼

JC

From a commercial shoot to publicize my book *Past Imperfect.*
▶

_JC_ Getting my star on the Walk of Fame in Hollywood was a tremendous honor and made for a day I shall never forget.

A lovely gesture from a fan.

JC This was my favorite picture at the time— one shot from a fashion shoot done in my home on Bowmont Drive, Beverly Hills.

ES

In a hangar at
Van Nuys airport
during an episode
of "Dynasty."

JC

1930s chic. I love this look.
I wish women could look like this
today, but it wouldn't be so easy
popping in and out of buses.

ES Joan's bathroom at Bowmont home.

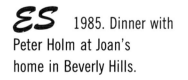 1985. Dinner with Peter Holm at Joan's home in Beverly Hills.

JC 1977—my gypsy look. I loved this home on Carolyn Way. It was made entirely of glass.

 Four young British girls making their way in Hollywood: Jane Seymour, Juliet Mills, Samantha Eggar, and myself, celebrating the Queen's Silver Jubilee—on the fourth of July, 1977.

JC One of my favorite art deco Lorenzi statues. Eddie found a clever use for her hoop. ▶

JC
I wish he'd move

that leaf.

JC That's better.

◂ *JC*

A hot day on *The Moneychangers'* set.

ES Brooding beauty, even dripping

wet, Joan still conveys that smoldering

magnetism.

Kim's Gym, Los Angeles, 1976. Joan splits.

JC People think this is easy.
My grandmother taught me this
when I was five years old, bringing
it back in style.

 On the rings
at Kim's Gym. ▶

JC A new form of torture.

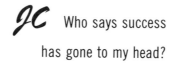 Who says success

has gone to my head?

ES Joan really fooled me. She had me keep this day free to shoot her line of hats at the house. Soon after I arrived, she suggested I sit down and have coffee. She then asked me if I'd like to fly to Las Vegas that evening. I still had no idea what was going on. Then Peter arrived in the room and hit me with the news—they were going to be married that night and asked if I would take their wedding pictures. The hat photographs turned out perfectly fine, but my mind was not really on the job that day.

JC In my house of mirrors— -1975.

JC
This photo was
used on the back
cover of *The Joan
Collins Beauty Book,*
published in 1978.
◄

 Having a wonderful time. Wish you were here.

JC This is the role that got me the part of Alexis. I worked for Aaron Spelling in 1981, playing Cleopatra in "Fantasy Island." When it came time to cast the role of Alexis, he remembered me in that part.

Cannes
Film
Festival,
1979.
The Stud
had just
opened.

JC In 1984 we launched the Joan Collins Jewelry Collection—some of my friends really loved it. In the photo are Corrinna Fields, Jackie Collins, Alex Mass, Shakira Caine, Keek Jourdan, Joanna Poitier, and Jolene Schatter.

ES Joan outglamourized thirty-five glamour girls from the *Playboy* Agency when she appeared with Paul Michael Glaser and David Soul on ''Murder on Playboy Island,'' a ''Starksy and Hutch'' episode filmed in July 1977 in Hawaii.

JC

I was amazed when they came from Madame Tussaud's in London to match my eyes.
They had boxes and boxes of green eyes of every possible shade.

ES
Midnight
—downtown
Los Angeles.
Making of
A Male Model,
TV film.

ES Tragically, this young man whose career started off with such promise died on the set of his TV series two years later. Jon-Erik Hexum had been picked from hundreds of hopeful young actors to play opposite Joan in this film.

JC
Katy with my
collection of
magazine
covers in
the Carolyn
Way house, 1967.

JC I thought I was pretty brave to go along with this. A series of photos about what actresses looked like without makeup was suggested and I agreed to do it with Eddie. Apparently, I was one of the few who did agree. Most of the others said they wouldn't be caught dead without their makeup. I see myself as an all-or-nothing person. I like myself either totally without makeup or totally with. I either wear T-shirts and no make-up or full make-up and smart clothes. It's the same with my hair. I either have to have it completely full or scraped back.

ES The picture was taken in Joan's trailer on the set at 6:30 in the morning before the makeup man arrived—and the camera can't lie—can it?

Like Dr. Linus Pauling, I believe in the power of the orange.

JC One shot from a fashion shoot done in my home on Bowmont Drive, Beverly Hills. ▶

JC Gold on silver, improvised with curtain material from the closet. ▼

ES

Leopard skin and fur. Fashion shoot at Bowmont home in Beverly Hills. ▲

JC
My first venture into producing and starring in a miniseries. Unfortunately, Eddie caught the moment I decided to blow a friendly raspberry at my co-star Gene Kelly. I was supposed to be sitting demurely in the balcony box, watching Gene conduct the orchestra in the Versailles Opera House.

JC This is not a pose for Eddie's camera. I'm actually dodging traffic around the Arc de Triomphe in Paris. As we were heading back to the hotel after a day's filming of "Sins" in Versailles, Eddie shouted at the driver to stop. Wondering what was wrong, I turned. Eddie was pointing to the Arc de Triomphe bathed in late afternoon sun and telling me what a great shot it would be with me in the middle of the Champs Elysees and traffic whizzing by. He was going to control the traffic and use strobe light. We didn't manage either of these things. Not only was Paris traffic not going to stop, but it could very well run us down. As we dashed back to the curb, Eddie managed to maneuver enough to grab this shot.

ES
"Sins" miniseries, 1985.

ES
A *fan-tasy* at the Golden Ball in Venice during the "Sins" miniseries shoot

(photo Sven Arnstein)

ES One of my favorite photos— Joan wearing the masquerade ball dress in "Sins."

 "Monte Carlo" miniseries, South of France, 1986.

JC   I don't usually
like frogs, but I did
take a shine to Kermit.

I love my bedroom in
beige, peach, and a
touch of jade green—
even without Kermit.

JC One of the very few pictures of the whole crew on the set of
"Dynasty," September 1986.

ES Joan wanted a photo of herself and the entire crew and production staff
together to give them as a Christmas card. She wanted to keep the card a surprise,
so she asked everyone to assemble just before lunch to get my shot for this book. I
had five minutes to get everyone together. People were still arriving as I started
shooting. After a couple of minutes everyone was so eager for lunch, the staircase
emptied as quickly as it had filled!

JC Venice, 1985. Celebrating Katy's thirteenth birthday with Tara and Sacha.

ES Joan's "Dynasty." It was a date to remember, Joan made sure of that. As a generous, loving mother, she turned her daughter Katy's thirteenth birthday in 1985 into a big happy family spectacular. Katy's party was held in a luxurious hotel in romantic Venice. There to join in the fun were Joan's children by second husband Anthony Newley: Tara, 20, and Sacha, 18.

JC I'm on a yacht and you're not— with daughter Tara on the Venice canals during the filming of "Sins" in 1985.

83 On location near Juniper, Florida, Joan risks encounters with alligators for realism in *Empire of the Ants*, a movie in which Joan and her co-stars flee into the swamps to escape a colony of giant ants. This sequence shows Joan—who insisted on doing her own stunts—taking the plunge into swamp water after an ant tips the boat over. (The ant was superimposed on the film later; two men in wetsuits did the real pushing.) To guard against alligator attacks, a rifleman was stationed just off-camera. Joan escaped being bitten by a gator, but she sustained cuts and bruises on submerged tree roots. It wasn't until she was out of the water that Joan, grimacing, began to feel the consequences of her realistic performance.

JC How they turned the "bitch" into a witch: It took Hollywood makeup men two and a half hours to turn me into an evil old hag. They used foam rubber, putty, false black teeth, long brown fingernails and a gray wig to transform me into the wicked witch for a TV version of the Hansel and Gretel fairy tale. The change was so startling that even my daughter Tara didn't recognize me.

ES Joan also plays the evil stepmother, a glamorous redhead in a peasant dress. But it was the role of the wicked witch that really delighted her, though she roasted under thick makeup when a heat wave hit Los Angeles during filming. As she sweated it out on location in a park, Joan found she had other little troubles. She had difficulty keeping her long rubber chin in place and her outsized nose meant that she couldn't eat for hours. All she could do was sip cool drinks through a straw.

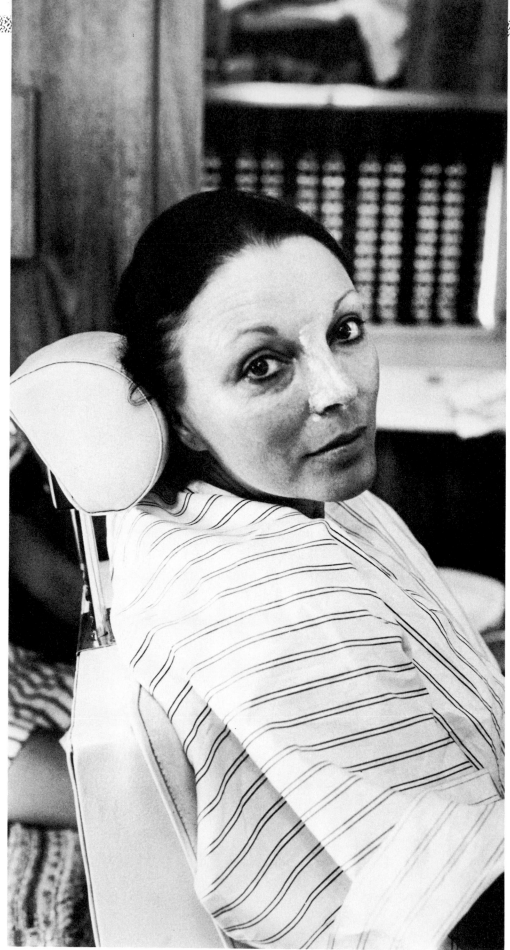

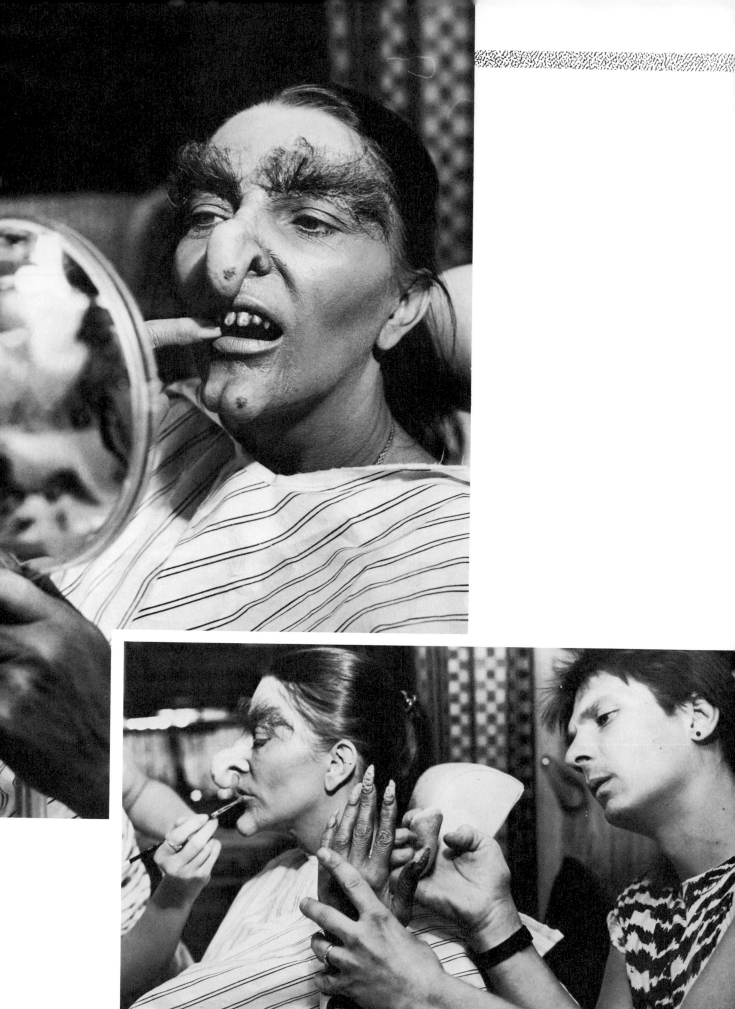

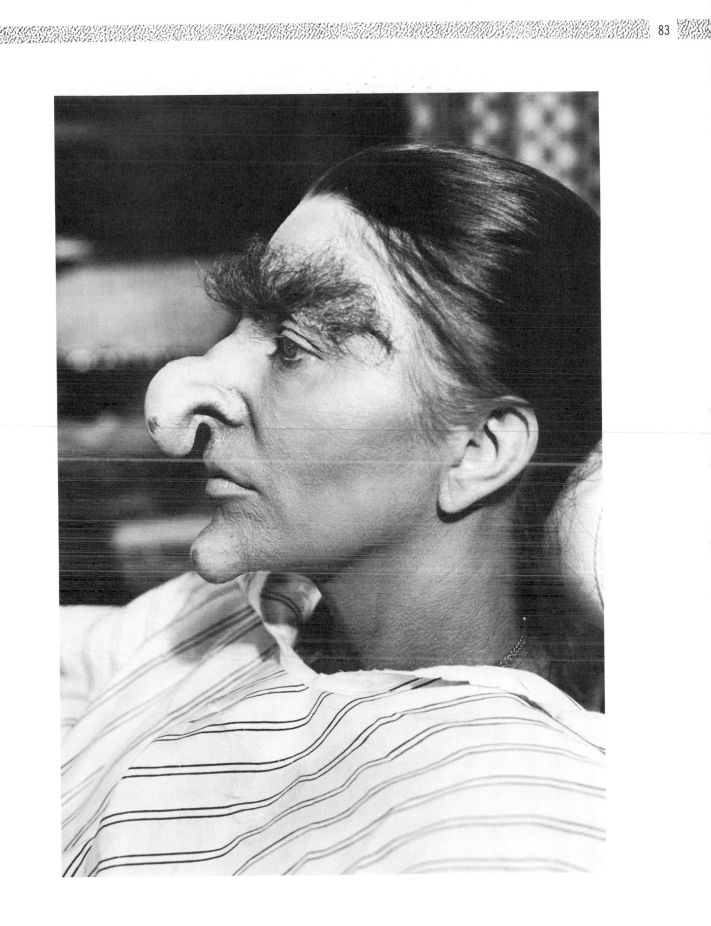

JC Moving house yet again.
Eddie was supposed to come over and
help me unload these boxes. Instead, he
insisted on taking photographs before we
unloaded and hung pictures.

How astute of the paint company to put this paper DYNASTAR hat in with the paint pots.

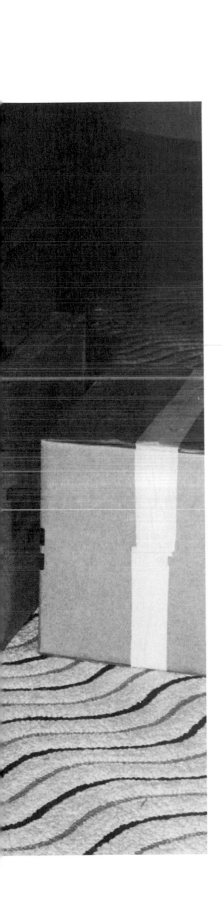

ES August, 1983. Peter Holm and Joan Collins. This is the first photograph of Joan and Peter together—taken on the back patio of Joan's house.

JC Fame at last. When they start selling T-shirts with this message on them, you known you've come a long way, baby! It reads: "Vicious, scheming, power-hungry—and successful."

This is my "girl Friday," Judy Bryer. Behind every successful woman is another successful woman, without whose presence things wouldn't function as well.

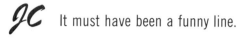 It must have been a funny line.

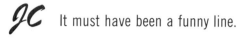 British royalty meets American royalty! Guests included Jeremy Irons, Stewart Granger, and Elizabeth Taylor.

JC Elizabeth Taylor and I are both wearing our Nolan Miller dresses in anticipation of meeting Princess Anne at a 1985 function for the British Film Institute in Los Angeles.

ES Elizabeth Taylor was just out of the Betty Ford Clinic and looked stunning.

DAILY MIRROR

er 5, 1981   12p

**Sophisticated
Lady Joan is
set to beat JR**

er quits
fast TV
baby

BELL

tzen has turned down a
third child is on the way.
er and her husband,
BBC executive
and Wilcox, already
wo young daughters
r, reportedly offered
a year by TV-AM,
oliday last night.

pull-out was
by Peter Jay,
TV-AM organisa-
begin broadcast-

sther is expect-
in November.
will be the
children all
s old.

involved
been just
r."

her-to-be,
expected
Rippon.
Robert
in the

SULTRY: Joan as the ex-wife who comes home to cause chaos.

EXCLUSIVE picture by EDDIE SANDERSON

VR'S

**She stars in
the show that
toppled Dallas**

ES Little did we know what was going to happen to Joan. This headline appeared in a British paper. That runaway success in "Dynasty" almost didn't happen. Joan was third choice for the role. The producers first approached Raquel Welch and then Sophia Loren. Both players turned down the offer.

JC Blake and Alexis—also just good friends—taken in the boardroom of our boss, Aaron Spelling.

JC September 1981. The first picture ever taken of me as Alexis. Eddie came to Twentieth Century Fox where we were shooting and said, "You look good in that hat. Let's shoot a couple of happy snaps." So we did this during lunch hour. It was ninety degrees in the shade and that suit is made of wool!

JC From the neck up, Alexis —from the neck down, another "Dynasty" crew member.

ES Even with a wedding veil and cowboy boots, it's just a normal day on Hollywood Boulevard.

JC Alexis marries for the third time in a little English country church in the quaint village of Mersham. At least, that's what the script said. In fact, though, the scene was shot in a church on Hollywood Boulevard, California, while scores of fans clustered around.

ES Observers on the set described Joan as breathtakingly beautiful in a full-length oyster satin gown with a sweetheart neck gathered at each shoulder by an antique art deco diamond clip pin. A tricornered hat decorated with lily of the valley and trailing three yards of white veiling tops things off.

JC I'm trying to find out what the boys in the back room will have, so I ask them in song. It's not exactly Marlene Dietrich's version, but the way Alexis would do it. My voice isn't going to cause Barbra Streisand to lose any sleep, but at least it's on key, and I'm proud I selected the song myself.

ES Joan makes her song- and-dance-girl debut at the age of 50.

ES Somehow, it's hard to imagine Joan Collins leading a cloistered life, but she turned up as a nun—and not for the first time—when Alexis, that unholy character, tried a disguise. It had been thirty years since Joan took off the habit and appeared as a fresh-faced nun opposite Richard Burton in the film *Seawife.* But she still has a certain heavenly quality.

JC Saint Joan. I don't think viewers ever expected to see Alexis disguised as a nun in this episode of "Dynasty" shot in January, 1986.

JC Queen for a day. This scene was eventually cut when audiences wrote in to tell how much they hated King Galen.

ES A well-controlled roll on "Dynasty," November 1986.

JC Whoever said "Dynasty" is just a glamour show was not on the set the day Diahann and I had the cat fight to end all cat fights.

JC Not my usual mode of travel.

ES A scene from ''Dynasty'' in which Joan gets to whizz around the streets on a 600cc motorbike. This scene was shot in the studio with trees and bushes in pots and artificial brick, providing a realistic look in a controlled situation.

JC Barbra, Tina, Diana—you don't have to worry!

ES In a Los Angeles recording studio, recording "The last time I saw Paris" for the miniseries "Monte Carlo."

JC George Hamilton and I had wanted to work together for many years before "Monte Carlo." This photo was taken when we were considering a project in 1978. ▶

JC The second miniseries I produced and starred in was "Monte Carlo," shot in the south of France during the spring of 1986 with George Hamilton, Malcolm McDowell—and Geoffrey Lane. When Eddie said he needed Geoffrey (my personal publicist) to hold part of a palm tree for background, little did Mr. Lane realize he would be in the photo.

JC Behind bars in "Monte Carlo," the second miniseries I produced and starred in. Shot in the South of France.

(Canada Dry commercial in Paris; Photo by Sven Arnstein)

JC I'm sure they'll never use this.
It's kind of a boring picture,
although you're in it.

JC This French roller skater couldn't believe her eyes when she saw me sitting outside the theater cafe in Versailles. We were shooting "Sins" in the Opera House next door.

JC Outside the entrance to the Casino on the banks of the Grand Canal in Venice. This is where we shot the Golden Ball sequence in "Sins." Peter Holm appeared in the mini-series as an announcer.

ES Quite a sight, watching Joan climb in and out of a Venice taxi (canal boat) three or four times a day in this dress.

JC
I must have
played more
seductive
queens
than any
actress in
history!

ES*.* Quite often the final picture doesn't tell the full story, for instance, showing the perfect forced smile five minutes after being clawed by a hawk with three-inch talons. Joan had a leading role in a science-fiction movie called *Fantastic Voyage* made in April 1977. She played the seductive queen of Halyana who ruled her subjects with the aid of a hawk.

JC   Winter 1981 at our house in England. My spare time is very precious and I like to spend as much of it as I can with Katy.

ES   A good sport—even after a trip in the English countryside—New Years' Day, 1981.

JC Time for celebration, New Years 1987, moving into my new house in Beverly Hills. Another of Eddie's five-minute cover shots.

ES A request for a New Year's cover of Joan from a German magazine turned into a nightmare. After spending an hour tying three dozen helium balloons in the lobby of Joan's house, Joan arrived home in the middle of a hectic day with only five minutes to spare for the picture. I'd only taken a few frames when the lights gave out on me. I frantically fiddled with the lights, but to no avail. With time running out, the only thing I could do was to attempt taking the picture by available light. By holding my breath and using a slow shutter speed, I managed to capture lots of movement as Joan threw streamers into the air. By this time balloons were drifting around the room, but careful cropping hides where they are tied to brass camels and ashtrays.

JC In my office at the factory. The phone on the right summons me to the set, the one on the left is for daily business routine.

ES "It's tiring just watching Joan talking on two phones . . . choosing accessories . . . autographing photographs . . . learning her lines—all at the same time!

Many of my photographs of Joan Collins may look as though they were shot in a studio, but I am not a studio photographer. Most of my work is done on the run. I carry my portable power packs and umbrellas along with me, although I much prefer shooting with available light. Some of my very favorite photographs of Joan have been taken in the strangest places, in less-than-favorable lighting conditions, but whatever the situation, Joan has been most understanding. She's a total professional. She knows what it takes to make a good photograph and is usually most cooperative.

There are those moments, of course, when even *I* wouldn't dream of disturbing her. These usually occur on a location when, during shooting breaks, Joan can occasionally be seen all wrapped up in a robe in her chair with her feet up on the dressing table, peering through her reading glasses at the English papers. "One of my few moments of peace," she calls this. I've cringed as I watched other photographers approach her in these tranquil moments, thinking that they've found the ideal time to whisk her away for a special shot. Sometimes she doesn't say a word. But if looks could kill . . . well! Even though I've photographed Joan in countless glamour situations, it can still take my breath away to see her descend the staircase from her dressing room wearing another of her stunning outfits, every inch the perfect model. Sometimes a few strange accessories . . . but I've got used to seeing Joan in a ten-thousand-dollar Valentino gold dress and Shocking Pink furry slippers.

Then it's down to work. I'm sure a lot of people think it's pretty easy to photograph someone as beautiful as Joan. It's not. Mentally, it's tough, constantly dealing with lighting exposures, facial angles, props, camera settings, and so on. It's also physically demanding.

Meanwhile, the subject needs attention too! I usually talk to Joan while I'm shooting. My rapport with her goes a long way in creating the mood for that particular shot. Our British sense of humor gets us over the occasional stumbling block.

A session can often last several hours, at the end of which I'm usually physically tired but emotionally high, the result of what I believe has been another successful shoot.

At this point Joan is still going strong, even though during the session, she has had to deal with hair; makeup; sitting in awkward positions; moving her body this way, that way; being told to turn her face "just an inch," head up a fraction, hand a little farther out, leg a little more bent, and a dozen more directions.

And what do I get for all this? A dazzling set of pictures that, once edited, will appear on magazine covers around the world.

*A*lthough it's exciting to photograph Joan the "star," and many people think of or visualize Joan Collins as Alexis in "Dynasty," it is Joan's diversity that has held my interest for the past fourteen years. If you know your subject well, you're able to make her reveal herself in different ways on film. During some of my sessions with Joan, I ask her about her daughter Katy, because she adores her, and watch her whole face simply light up. But just mention swamp creatures and I'll have an open-mouth shot destined for the trash!

Because Joan and I work together so often, I'm constantly challenged to come up with new ideas and approaches. Joan is a great help in this area, suggesting everything from new wardrobe ideas to accessories for herself dressed as a nun.

In the fourteen years that I have known Joan, I have seen the many facets of her personality, both professional and personal. I have seen her painting the house and attending premieres, knee deep in both Florida swamp mud and million-dollar fashions, clawed by hawks and luxuriating on sumptuous furs.

One thing Joan Collins isn't, and that's slow to come to the point—but it's the professionalism that makes her want to do everything right. Joan learned a lot from the "Alexis" character. It taught her how to be more assertive, to be strong in business, and how not to tolerate things she doesn't like. She has tremendous strength. She is a survivor and has a keen sense of humor.

*J*oan strives always to stay one step ahead in fashion. According to a 1986 poll, Joan is Great Britain's most stylish woman outside the Royal Family.

But doesn't she get fed up having to look her best all the time? "No" she says. "Being at my dressing table in the morning gives me some time to myself. I have my cassette player and a mini-recorder to make notes . . . though some mornings I wish it were Saturday so I could relax." Nevertheless, Joan needs little sleep, and has abundant energy. "Energy," Joan believes, "begets energy. If you work really hard and enjoy your work, it makes you more energetic."

Often she leaves home at six in the morning and sometimes doesn't get back until nine at night.

Joan is careful about her diet, smokes only occasionally, exercises regularly, drinks a little wine or champagne, and that's about it. She adds, "I've never had the slightest desire to get involved in drugs or heavy boozing. I just hate drugs, and I've been extremely strong with my children about that."

Joan has collected a houseful of beautiful things, not all expensive, but all with taste and style. And she has put them together to create a home that reflects her own sparkling personality, but also, as in her peach-colored bedroom, reflects the softness within her.

oan Collins is still very much her own person. Life is very good for her right now. Her 14-year-old daughter, Katy, is at school in England. Joan is closer to her two older children, Sacha and Tara, than ever before; she has security and cash and the temperament to enjoy spending it—and she's shrewd enough to know that if she plays her cards right, makes her own decisions, and listens to her own voice of experience, then the future will be bright indeed. Her epitaph, she once said, would hopefully read, "She had her cake and ate it too."

I value Joan's friendship outside the professional arena and greatly respect the trust she places in me.

I hope the relationship we have continues, and that we can both enjoy creating more <u>Portraits of a Star.</u>